BALANCE

BALANCE

CHRISTOPHER WARD

Order this book online at www.trafford.com
or email orders@trafford.com

Most Trafford titles are also available at major online book retailers.

Printed in the United States of America.

ISBN: 978-1-4669-2189-4 (sc)
ISBN: 978-1-4669-2190-0 (hc)
ISBN: 978-1-4669-2191-7 (e)

Library of Congress Control Number: 2012905581

Trafford rev. 03/22/2012

 www.trafford.com

North America & international
toll-free: 1 888 232 4444 (USA & Canada)
phone: 250 383 6864 ♦ fax: 812 355 4082

This book is dedicated to my family and friends who supported me through some pretty dark times. To my friends, I thank you for caring in the rough times and treating me like nothing was ever wrong when I returned. (And thanks for being my editor, Heather!)

To my parents, I may not be here at all today if it wasn't for you. I will never be able to repay you for your unwavering love.

And to my love Lori, you were my rock when I couldn't stand on my own. You are simply amazing.

It's always interesting to see who is holding the light for you when you are stuck in the middle of the tunnel. I love you all.

THE INTRO . . .

I told my wife I thought it was time for me to write a book. She asked, "What about?" I told her I wasn't quite sure yet, but I've seen a lot of stuff—good and bad. And through those experiences, I think I have some knowledge I could pass on to others that could possibly benefit them. That's really it.

She then asked me, "So what are you going to call it?" I replied with, "Who cares?" I'll figure that out later. I told her I'd think I'd call it "No BS" . . . which could mean a couple of things. The first one is pretty obvious: no bullshit. You should know now that I have a tendency to occasionally use vulgarity. If that offends you, stop reading now. I won't be dropping the f-bomb in this book. I may be thinking it, but I won't put it in print (you know, for the kids' sake.) But I once had someone I admire tell me that when I'm trying to be politically correct, I'm really "obtuse." After I went back to my desk and realized he wasn't calling me an angle—the only time I'd heard that word was back in high school math—I got pissed. Of course, he just wanted me to speak my mind in meetings, not use vulgarity. But I've taken the creative liberty to do both. Oh yeah, my other meaning for "No BS" means "No Borders Society." But you can read about that one later.

Anyway, that little rant should give you a feel for how the rest of this book is going to go. I tell stories inside of other stories. But just when you think I've gone way off track, I'll bring it back. Trust me.

Here's something else you should know. I'm writing this book like I like to read, because something is wrong if I can't tolerate reading my own book. So here's the deal. You should be able to read most of the following chapters as their own independent stories. Why? Because I do my best reading on the toilet. It really frustrates me when I don't want to put down a book but I'm forced to because my legs have fallen asleep and I've been done pooping for 30 minutes. I also picked this format because my mind flies around at a ridiculous speed. I talk fast and switch topics frequently. I have a lot to say and plenty of people to entertain, wear out or annoy. I also don't think I have enough knowledge about any one subject to warrant an entire book. So if you are looking for 200 pages of tight content with twists and turns that require you to analyze each page, I'd suggest using this book to prop up that shaky leg on your couch. If you want to be entertained in short doses and hopefully can benefit from a few of the things I have to say, then read on.

Oh yeah, back to that title. As you know if you read the cover, I've decided on "Balance." I thought the title would come to me later as I wrote this thing, but I've determined "balance" is the key to me living a productive life. I'm not saying it is for you, but it is for me. I may have to call Van Halen to see if they are OK with it, because I admit that I borrowed it from an old album of theirs. I was a Sammy Hagar Van Halen fan, by the way. But anyway, that "balance" theme will find its way into just about every story in the coming pages.

You will also see a recurring character throughout various parts of this book. It's a guy I know who has battled bipolar disorder off and on over the past 15 years. If anyone needs balance in his life, it's this dude. I like him though, and he tells a good story. OK, I'll end the suspense—it's me. My original plan was to tell my entire story in third person about my friend "Ron," only to reveal at the end that the character was really me. But that's been done before, so I'll just tell you up front. I'm bipolar. (Insert daunting music here.) In fact, I actually began writing this book when I was on the manic side of the disease. So as you read this you may find some points where I sound really self-righteous. I was pretty manic during those parts as I wrote from a stream of consciousness usually at 3 or 4 a.m. Now that I'm back to healthy and level, I thought about going back and rewriting some of those parts. But that's the whole point, right? I want people to see how I'm thinking when I'm manic and hopefully others who are dealing with bipolar can relate and feel some comfort that others deal with the same demons.

Anyway, I'll use my experiences, opinions and issues with bipolar to make my points. And like I said, maybe I can help someone out there with similar issues. I'll balance the serious story with some lighthearted stuff I'll throw in between. So buckle up folks, and prepare to enter the warped circus of my mind. And make sure you wipe after you finish up what you've been doing. (Oh yeah, I like poop jokes too.)

For those who would like to read my rants only or at least start with them, go to the following chapters: 1-3, 5-7, 9-11, 16 and 18-21.

If you'd like to follow my story of battling with bipolar only, go to these chapters: 4, 8, 12-15, 17 and 22-27. Yes, I bounce back and forth all over the place. Remember I'm bipolar. (That's a joke, of course.)

1

No BS
(This is the No Bullshit Part)

I decided to start with this one as I once told a co-worker I should write a book called "No BS Communications." I forgot to tell you in that exciting intro I'm a marketing and communications manager by trade. I have a degree in public relations with a minor in marketing from Kent State University (KSU). I'd like to start there, as the education I received gave me the foundation to start what I feel has been a successful career so far. (And yes, for those of you outside of Northeast Ohio, it's the school where the kids were shot during a Vietnam War protest in 1970. I won't address that any further in this book.)

While at KSU, I had a professor named Bill Sledzik. He led the PR program at Kent and is still at Kent today. He's also now a well-known PR blogger. But I digress. Bill had real-world experience from running his own PR firm and working in the field for a long time before becoming a professor. I learned a lot from him, and he helped me get the job I'm in today. It was supposed to be a three-month internship, and I've been with the company more than 12 years now. Longest internship ever. The HR guy still looks at me funny when I walk by. I'm like the dude on "Office Space" with the stapler issue. (Oh yeah, one more thing. I'll make references to movies and TV shows I like. If you don't get a reference, look it up as it's probably some funny stuff.)

Anyway, many things have changed in communications and PR since I left KSU in 2000. Now everyone can report the news. If you have a cellphone and the ambition to snap a picture of pretty much anything, you can get it on the Web. Social media was just getting rolling when I finished school, so I didn't learn how to deal with that from Bill. I'll talk about social media later anyway, or I'll tweet you about it. (If you don't know what that means, Google it. If you don't know what "Google it" means, crawl out from under that rock so you have enough light to read this book.)

What I learned from Bill was simple. Do the right thing, and be a good person. If your company did something wrong or made a mistake, own it. Don't hide. Take responsibility. Tell people what happened and how you are going to fix it. Treat people like adults. If you are working with employees, don't feed them corporate bullshit. They don't want to hear about "synergy" and crap like that. They want to know if their jobs are going to be there tomorrow and if their 401(k) is coming back. Treat your employees with respect so they become true ambassadors for your company. If something is bullshit, call it bullshit and try to fix it. Don't call it an opportunity and tell people we need to "get on the same page" and find a "win-win situation."

That's pretty much it. Of course Bill stated these things much more eloquently than that, but I think you get the point. Find the balance between being positive, while being genuine and realistic. Treat people like you would like to be treated. Deliver bad news yourself. Tell your story. Don't let others tell it for you. That sounds pretty simple to me. Now you see why I didn't try to write an entire book on this one.

2

The Other "No BS"

I came up with this "No Borders Society" concept in January 2010 when I was ranting in a weekly email I used to send to our sales force at work. (If someone else has coined this phrase, send a note to my lawyer.) Anyway, I like the way I wrote it then—so a slightly revised version is below. I took out the internal, company stuff you wouldn't get. Stick with me through the beginning of the story, as it will get to the point. For reference, this occurred right after the horrible earthquake rocked Haiti in 2010.

"I was out of town and got the opportunity to meet with a colleague I've worked with for a couple of years via phone and email. Her name is Lisa. We were supposed to meet for lunch, but she had to change our plans to only meet at her desk for about 30 minutes as she was swamped with work. Why? Because she works in corporate social responsibility for a transportation company and coordinates most of the shipping

the company donates. She coordinated a number of full 727 aircraft of donated goods for delivery into Haiti. With limited landing rights in Haiti and thousands of requests, she was a bit overwhelmed but was handling everything beautifully with a smile on her face. You only need to talk to her for about five seconds to see that she has a good heart and just wants to help people. From her small cubicle, her work has benefitted thousands (if not millions) of people over her career. When things don't go right, she fixes them. And on highly visible shipments when things don't go right, she receives calls from senior executives (very senior). But again, she handles those calls with a smile as well and quickly reassures everyone that everything is going to be fine.

When it's all said and done, it doesn't matter where Lisa works. She'll find a way to help and serve others. She doesn't want the recognition, just the feeling that she's positively impacting others. I think I'm a better person after spending those 30 minutes with her, listening to the passion she has for helping those in need. And she has it right. It's all about helping others when you can.

This brings me to my movie-watching experience this week. (I know, bad transition.) Anyway, I watched "The Hurt Locker," which follows a three-man squadron in Iraq that is called in to diffuse bombs. If you haven't seen it, I'd recommend you rent it. I won't ruin it for you, but the same theme was in it that I saw with Lisa. In a much different way, the squadron was dedicated to helping others—their fellow soldiers and the civilians in Iraq, most of whom are good people. The people of Iraq aren't the enemy. The people who strap the bombs to the chest of an innocent family man and use him as a human bomb . . . they are the enemy, and those people could be in Iraq or right here in the U.S. They are the enemy of a global society whose members should look out for and help each other. And that society should be borderless. It's a No Borders

Society—and the only requirements to get in are to be a good person, help others and be selfless instead of selfish.

Anyway, the conflicts I'm seeing in the world and in business seem to be driven by personal agendas, not by what's best for the greater good. If everybody spent a little more time looking out for others like Lisa does, and a little less time self-promoting, we'd all be better off.

So that's what I wrote back then, but I'd like to take this No Borders Society idea a bit further. With the global connectivity that's now available thanks to the Internet, the world has become much smaller. It's not "us versus them." Don't get me wrong, I love America and the freedoms we have. But don't you think everyone should be entitled to those same freedoms? You can't control where you are born or who you parents are. If you are lucky enough to escape a terrible environment, shouldn't we as human beings be open to helping you? I hear people say, "Close our borders." Well guess what? There are plenty of good people coming in from other countries who are working hard and making a positive impact on our society. There are also plenty of assholes who were born and raised in the U.S. who are lazy and a drain on society.

I won't take this any further, as I think I've made my point. It's not the U.S. versus Iraq or Afghanistan or even terrorism. It's the people with good intentions against the people with bad intentions. In my borderless society, I'll take the people with good intentions—and I don't care where you live or what you believe. That's not any of my business. Worship how you please, and think and live freely. For those people with bad intentions who hurt other people to push their personal agendas, you are the enemy. And one day I hope the citizens of the No BS declare war on you . . . instead of each other.

3

What's On My iPod?

For those of you reading this book in order, I admit that was some serious stuff back there in chapter 2. So let's take a deep breath and talk about some brainless stuff, such as what's on my iPod right now. I have 235 songs on there as of today.

I use my iPod primarily when I'm working out, so I have a limited number of bands I really like that play music that motivates me in the gym. Those bands include:
Metallica, Stone Temple Pilots, Linkin Park, Godsmack, Eminem, 3 Doors Down, Foo Fighters, Rob Zombie, The Beastie Boys (old school, baby) and more.

Stone Temple Pilots is my favorite band of all time. The band's songs can rock it out or slow it down and make you think. Scott Weiland (the lead singer) is a pretty talented dude with some balance issues of his own—better known as a history of drug addiction. I'll give him credit though; he openly admits his mistakes and has tried to make his life better. I respect that. We all have our own crosses to bear, right? At least he had the guts to take his skeletons out of the closet. Enough said there. You can read his book if you want to learn more. It's one of the few books I read in less than two days.

I do want to address one more thing for you people out there who stopped on a dime when you read "Godsmack." Before you accuse me of worshiping the dark one, let me explain. I once listened to an interview with the members of the band, and they explained how they got their name. Apparently before the band even had a name, one of the members showed up for a rehearsal with a big cold sore on his lip. Another member of the band said, "Man, God smacked you with that one," or something to that effect. The rest, as they say, is history.

And as for my final thoughts on music, I've always like "speed metal" and heavy metal music. I know some of you are thinking "what an asshole" or once again, "he must worship Satan." That's not the case. Maybe I'm an asshole, but I've learned that I'm a big follower of Jesus (see chapters 5 and 6). Anyway, my first concert was a Pantera show and I loved it. They were loud, screamed unrecognizable lyrics and their guitars and drums flew at a feverish pace. Their songs seemed to give me energy. The bottom line is I don't even know the lyrics to most of the metal songs I listen to. They could be screaming, "READ THE BIBLE, BRUSH YOUR TEETH, EAT SQUARE MEALS, PUPPIES ARE CUTE, GET YOUR COLON CHECKED . . . AHHHHHHHHHHH!" I just don't' care what they are saying. I just like the music. So if you are one of those people out there who wants to blame music lyrics or video games for your children's mistakes, why don't you take a look in the mirror? You may just find the real, negative influencing force in there.

Oh yeah, I also have a couple of Justin Timberlake songs on my iPod too. Don't judge me, that guy is talented. And like I said, it's all about balance for me. And who doesn't want to bring sexy back?

4

"The Worst Joke Ever"— My Story Begins

I'm going to get serious again. Like I said, it turns out I was diagnosed with manic depression or bipolar disorder . . . we'll go with bipolar for future references. (There's a Stone Temple Pilots song called Bi-polar Bear, so we'll go with that descriptive term.)

Anyway, I was just a regular boy growing up. I had good parents who taught me to respect others, work hard and just be a good person. And I think I did that. I was a straight-A student, had lots of friends, was pretty good at sports and stayed out of trouble.

Behind closed doors, I was constantly worried about everything and blew little things way out of proportion. I put too much pressure on myself while also wanting to make sure everyone else was happy too. I was a time bomb, but I didn't know it.

By the time I got to high school, things were still good. The grades were still A's, and I was going to be a varsity athlete in a couple of sports. By the beginning of my junior year, things were even better. I just got my driver's license and had my first "real" girlfriend. Then things took a turn for the worse. I became increasingly tired and just couldn't get my mind around what was going on. Everything began to feel like a monumental task—school, basketball practice, having a girlfriend. I couldn't understand how I could have all of these great things and feel so terrible every day. I really liked my new girlfriend but tried to break it off with her, as I didn't want to drag her into whatever the hell was going on with me. She understood, supported me and said she'd be waiting when I figured things out. (She did, which was pretty mature for a freshman in high school. But hey, I was a good-looking kid. Ha ha.)

One day I decided I wasn't getting out of bed. That was the only place I felt any peace. My mind could wander, and I could drift in and out of consciousness. And no one would have to deal with how I was feeling. Of course, I had those parents who didn't align to that plan. My mom said I had two choices: get up and go to school or go to the doctor/hospital. I chose the hospital . . . not because I felt like I needed to go. I just couldn't stand the thought of being around the other kids in school. I was always the one talking to everyone and goofing around, but I just couldn't do it. I couldn't concentrate. I felt tired and confused. And I didn't have any idea why. So the hospital sounded better than high school.

What I didn't realize is that when you go to a hospital and refuse to talk to anyone to prove how bad you feel, that doesn't work so well. What it does do is land you in the psychiatric ward. If I had known that's the "hospital" I would have landed in, I may have thought better about that decision earlier in the day to not go to school. In fact, I also think I had a chance during the discussion with a psychiatrist to avoid it. The doctor asked, "So have you ever thought about killing yourself?" To that point in my life, I had never really thought about that before—so I said nothing and shrugged my shoulders. That was enough for the doctor to write his "reservation for one" for a stay on the psychiatric floor. I still wonder if I would have just said "no" to that question, if I would have been riding back home with my parents that night.

So in the span of literally a month, I went from the guy walking across the football field as the junior class homecoming court representative (as voted on by the other students) to the kid in the hospital rumored to have been thinking about killing himself. Talk about no balance. That's one end of the spectrum to the other.

I spent about four or five days in the hospital, getting tons of tests run on my body and brain to make sure nothing was physically wrong. I can't remember exactly how many days I was in there. I do remember sitting by the window on a Friday night counting cars as they drove by on the highway below, wondering how I got here instead of being a normal kid hanging out with this friends. It was a horrible feeling.

I got out the day before Thanksgiving, which bought me a couple of extra days before I had to face the music of high school again. When I got out, my girlfriend was the first to call to see how I was doing. I didn't want to talk to her and said I'd call her that Sunday. I didn't, and I learned later that she sat around the entire day waiting for me to call. I just didn't know what to say and was embarrassed. I also was busy trying to figure out how I could avoid school on Monday.

So, about that joke. I did return to school that Monday and felt the eyes peering through me as I moped down the halls—at least it felt that way to me. I refused to join the basketball team although the head coach left a spot for me on the roster. I sat through one practice before Christmas break to see if I could do it, but even watching was a chore. I just wanted to lie on the couch and escape whatever was screwing me up. So that's what I did for all of December and most of January. The doctors told me I was suffering from clinical depression, and medication would pull me out. But there was one doctor who was not very nice to me. Like I said, my defense mechanism was to not talk at all . . . to anyone. I didn't have answers to anyone's questions, the biggest one being: why are you depressed? What's wrong? So I didn't talk. I also spent more time trying to figure out how they were trying to draw inaccurate conclusions from analyzing the questions they were asking instead of actually letting them help me. But I didn't deserve what one doctor gave me. After a session with him asking questions and me responding by just shrugging my shoulders or shaking my head, the frustrated doctor gave a quick debriefing to my parents while I was standing there, listening to the conversation.

My mom asked if there were any other doctors who could possibly help me. The doctor replied with, "Yeah, maybe Dr. Kevorkian." (For those of you who may be younger, Dr. Kevorkian was the "suicide doctor" who helped ailing people kill themselves through some type of euthanasia.)

Luckily, I was not impacted by this idiot doctor's comment. In fact, all I could think was, "I can't believe he just said that. What if I were a kid with real problems who heard that and then went and killed myself? I'm guessing my parents would get a helluva check out of that lawsuit." I also realized that the first time I ever thought about the idea of killing myself was when the previous therapist introduced it.

And that, my friends, is the worst joke ever in my opinion. More from my "highs and lows" with bipolar and my pursuit of balance later in the book. Why balance? Because I battled extreme lows and then extreme highs for nearly three years before finally being diagnosed with bipolar disorder. Every time I got depressed, the answer from those fine psychiatrists was antidepressants. Unfortunately the drugs were the ones that helped to push bipolar people to the manic side. And I wasn't mature enough at the time to recognize it and self-regulate it. Every time it happened, people were just happy that I was energetic—extremely energetic—but mostly back to my old self. They were willing to endure some of my unusual behavior just to have me back and seeming to enjoy life. Unfortunately, that was a dangerous ride. But like I said, more on that later.

5

I'm Going to Church in an Hour, and I'm Disenchanted With Organized Religion

That title probably caught your attention. Some of the self-righteous hypocrites are chomping at the bit to call me blasphemous. I invite it, as I can defend my opinions. Here goes.

Growing up, I rarely went to church, besides on Easter, Christmas and . . . well that's pretty much it. I was always uncomfortable when my Catholic friends talked about going to Bible study classes on Wednesday nights, but mostly I just stayed quiet. Now that I'm older, I look back and I'm glad it happened that way. My mom and dad have worked hard their entire lives, and Sunday was the one day they could sleep in a little bit and relax. Even God rested on the seventh day, right?

So let me make this clear. I believe in God, Jesus Christ and the Holy Spirit. But I've gotten there on my own terms. I've read some books, done some online research and started reading the Bible on my own. I've listened to everyone's opinions and have pretty much kept my mouth shut. I know there are good churches out there that truly teach about the principles of living the right way. I have an issue with those churches and religions that are close-minded, work harder to point out what's wrong with everything instead of what's great about them and have parishioners who are hypocrites. Besides that, I'm cool with religion.

I'm guessing most people choose their religion because their parents were that religion. When you are a kid, you don't have a choice, and many people simply don't feel the need to change when they become adults. Don't get me wrong, I'm sure many people have benefitted from their parents making informed decisions on how they've chosen to worship. I'm also guessing, in many cases, that decision turns out to be the one a child would make anyway when he or she becomes an adult. Then there are the others who have never taken the time to learn the differences between what people believe and why. It's easier to just say, we're right in our religion and you are wrong. I don't dig it.

Some of the biggest hypocrites I know go to church every Sunday. And some of the people with the biggest hearts I know, never go. Do I know what's right? Nope. I can only control what I do and be open to understanding why others do and believe as they do. It's not a matter of who's right. It's a matter of understanding the basic principles of Christianity and living them. Live the golden rule. Help others. Be selfless, not selfish. Help people when they ask for it. Don't be a hypocrite.

I'm sure some of you are steaming right now and screaming, "But wait, you say don't be a hypocrite, but then you also say you are about to go to church. What gives?" So here's the deal. I love to play basketball. When I'm feeling really good (and maybe even a bit manic), I play five to six times a week. At one gym, I started playing with a guy who plays a very good point-guard position. He is always looking for the open man and has great court vision. He's kind of balding, not in the greatest shape and always has this look of confidence on his face when he plays. In fact, the first two times I played against him, I was annoyed for some reason. And then when I played with him, I wasn't thrilled to share the point-guard role with him . . . until I saw him start passing. He has better court vision than I do. That is key to being a point guard. I'm now cool with going to the shooting-guard spot when I play with him.

One day we walked out of the building together after he had just thanked another guy and me for playing with him and said how much fun it was to play with people who get out and run. He asked me if I was off to work, and I said yeah. I asked him if he was on vacation or something, as it sounded like he didn't have to work from the tone of his voice. But he said he just didn't have any meetings until 10:30. I said, "Oh, what do you do?" He said, "I'm a minister." I said, "No kidding." Then I told him a little about what I just wrote . . . how I'm not the biggest fan of what I see in some religions, how I never went to church as a kid and how it always made me uncomfortable. I then asked what religion was practiced at his church. He said, "We're nondenominational. I don't like putting people in boxes." I inquired if I could just show up the following Sunday and he said, "Sure, come check it out. We have two sermons, 9:30 and 10:45. I'd suggest 10:45." I'm still not sure if that was a shot about me wanting to sleep in, but it sounded good anyway. So that's that. It is now 9:25 on that Sunday morning. I'll let you know how it goes. That may just be chapter 6.

6

So It Turns Out Religion
is OK in My Book . . .

To say the least, my experience at the church I mentioned in chapter 5 was a good one. If you haven't read chapter 5 yet, that's OK, but you may want to check it out before you read this one. Anyway, I still don't like religious leaders taking their interpretations of things and pushing them down their congregation members' throats. But I can choose to not be a part of those groups. But as I just read in Matthew, any place where more than two people gather to worship Jesus will find Him there . . . or something like that. I'll need to go back and check that line, or better yet, you do it if you want to check my reference. Either way, I found a church that is the way I always thought church should be. My wife liked it too. So we will back next week.

I'm not going to preach any further on this one, as I found the right preacher who can do that for me. And for those who are saying I'm now a hypocrite for changing my mind so quickly, I disagree. My former boss (Joel) once told me you are allowed to change your mind when you gather better information. Stubborn people who refuse to budge after they realize their initial decision could be improved usually fail or look foolish. I agree. (Thanks for the help, Joel . . . at least you know I was listening sometimes.)

7

My Travel Adventures

I use to write a weekly "article" in our sales newsletter at work. It was called "In Closing," and I would rant about everyday things. Usually I would talk about my cat and dog or sports. But often I had a story to tell after I had gone on a business trip. It turns out that people in the sales force and others in our company really seemed to enjoy these stories, so I figured I'd share some with you, because hey, here's another chapter I don't have to write off of the top of my head. So here goes.

Doing the Dance . . .

I was flying home from Memphis in one of those really roomy regional jets. At 5'5" tall, you know there's a space issue if I'm cramped in a plane. Anyway, I had a large beverage before boarding and, with nature calling, I was pumped to hear the "you can get up" ding when we got to cruising altitude. Unfortunately I was in the front of the plane, and the beverage cart had already beaten me to the aisle. I thought about diving over the top but decided that may be a bit risky in today's environment, plus I don't have the physical skills to do so. So I waited it out.

When the cart finally cleared, some guy jumped up and got to the restroom before I could even stand. Then once I stood up, a lady saw I was heading for pay dirt and cut me off. She then proceeded to take 20 minutes in there. Seriously, the flight attendant came back to ask if I heard "anything moving" in there. Despite the array of answers I had in my head, I decided to just shrug my shoulders. Anyway, there is a happy ending to my story as she was OK, and I was able to take care of business. The point of all this is that I'd much rather be here doing this (writing as part of my job) and hopefully providing people with info they can use. It sure beats doing the "pee-pee" dance in a crowded plane.

It's Easier When Your Luggage Arrives When You Do

My experience with my airline this week was not so good. To quickly summarize, my first flight through Atlanta cancelled and the re-route through Cincinnati was overbooked, but we (a co-worker and I) eventually made it about six hours late. My luggage arrived about 15 hours after that. I'll spare you the rest of the details, but I did learn the following things to share with you in case you are caught in a similar situation:

1. The guy at 9:55 p.m. at the baggage claim center does not care that you don't have clothes. I don't think his glare was a sign of sympathy.

2. The complimentary toiletries provided by the hotel are a nice touch, but the "toothbrush" has a similar structure to a cooked spaghetti noodle.
3. The complimentary hand/body lotion can serve as a substitute for aftershave in a pinch, but I would not recommend it.
4. The free disposable razor will literally tear the skin off of your face if you aren't careful. You may also miss a few spots.
5. The complimentary hand/body lotion is not a good substitute for hair gel.
6. There is something to be said for a fresh pair of . . . never mind.

My First Visit to Title Town

(For the context of this story to make sense, keep in mind that I'm a die-hard Pittsburgh Steelers fan. I also root for the Cleveland Indians and Cleveland Cavaliers.)

My travel took me to the worst place on earth for a sports fan who isn't a Red Sox fan . . . Boston on World Series parade day. A better name could have been, "The Sax are the greatest frickin' team in the history of America's pastime, hands down, no questions asked . . . we are wicked awesome" Day. I believe my local sales manager I was visiting intentionally had me meet him at a restaurant littered with televisions showing only the victory parade. He smiled and pointed at the players' antics while I tried not to lose my lunch. Every customer we visited had on some sort of Red Sox garb. Ah . . . I take that back, one guy had on a New England Patriots "we rule the football world" shirt.

I just wanted to "git in the cah" and drive home.

To add insult to injury, we then attended an event at the Patriots stadium. But those fans weren't nearly as full of themselves . . . yeah right. For a moment I thought I sensed sympathy as one guy told me to tell the Clevelanders to hang in there because the Pats went through years of struggling too. Then he yelled, "But now we are the cream of the crap!" (crop). Seriously, he screamed it . . . people looked. He then pounded his chest and punched me in the stomach. OK he didn't punch me, but I would have welcomed it. He then proceeded to tell me how he gave his big-screen TV to his son so he could make room for his new plasma because, and I quote, "That's the kind of TV you need to watch championships on, but Cleveland wouldn't know about that, huh?" I countered by asking if he had ever used my company before. He said, "Yeah, you guys are fast, but nat wicked fast like a Beckett fastball or Brady's laser arm." At that point, I surrendered and cried away the rest of the evening in my chowda.

8

"My Worst Day"—
My Story, Part 2

Getting back to my run with bipolar, when we left off I had just gotten through my first "depression" episode. What came next was the other "pole." It was a wild ride of endless energy where I talked fast, felt invincible and left people in my wake. I cycled back and forth from low to high and back again for nearly three years before finally being diagnosed correctly.

Of course there were plenty of things I regretted in retrospect. Some things I've written off to being out of my control, as I wouldn't do them when things are "normal." But there was one day I wished I could have had back. It's not necessarily the day I landed in a hospital or the day I flipped my car or one of the seemingly endless days of depression. It was one day in particular toward the end of my manic madness when I got into a dispute with my dad at my parents' home. (I had temporarily moved out at the time.) I had stopped by to grab what was left of my cash (a box of change) and tried to slip back out of the house. My dad tried to stop me from leaving, and a verbal battle ensued. It concluded with me running to my car and locking the doors. My father followed me to the car and tried to plead with me to get out and get help. I replied by extending my middle finger and pressing it against the glass in ignorant defiance. I then tore off out of the driveway.

Looking back, it felt like someone else was at the wheel at the time (literally and figuratively). But of all the rough days I've had with depression, I would take all the pain again for a chance to get that day back. My dad knows that outburst "wasn't me" and is just happy that I'm a happy, healthy guy today. But it still lingers in my memory. If you ever see me with my dad today, playing golf or just joking around, you can see why I feel this was the lowest of the low for me. Thank God I have the parents I have. I honestly don't know where I'd be today without them or even if I'd be here at all.

9

I'd Like to Give the Clock Back

Ever since I was a kid, I've always been my hardest critic. I expect perfection in everything I do, even though I know that's impossible. I also am a chronic worrier . . . so much so that my first-grade class labeled me "Mr. Worry." And thanks to the people who used to write those books, there was some little blue circle character to help educate kids about "worry." (Along with Mr. Happy, Mr. Sad, etc.) But hey, I'll wear that one. I try not to worry about things as much anymore, but I have to fight to keep those thoughts out of my mind.

So back to that "Mr. Worry" thing. I have a ridiculous level of self-consciousness that goes with it. This dates back to some of my earliest memories. I really think I had anxiety issues as a kid, but who the hell knows anymore. Anyway, I remember taking a spelling test in kindergarten. The brain buster of a word was "dress." For the life of me, I could not think of how it was spelled, so I did the unthinkable and looked off of my "neighbor's" paper. She had it right. (Sorry, April. It only happened once.) After we graded the papers, I couldn't stand what I had done and went up to talk to the teacher. Choking back tears, I told her about my horrible act. She told me it was great to be honest and she would just count that one wrong, but would give me the points for the rest of my correct answers. I was so relieved.

So what the hell does that have to do with a clock? Well let's fast-forward to when I was 15 years old. My best friend, Jimmy O., and I were playing in a junior golf tournament. The format consisted of a number of tournaments at local courses. You gained points for placing at each tournament with the top players from each age bracket—moving on to the championship round for an 18-hole, winner-takes-all tournament. You could cut the drama with a knife. (Sarcastic tone intended there.)

I already felt bad about winning one tournament and tying for first in another. (I actually got second after losing in a playoff.) I was in the 13-15 year-old age bracket, while my friends were all in the 16-18 division. I have a late July birthday, and your division was determined by your age at the start of the "tour."

Anyway, when the big championship day came, I was on my A-game. We were playing at the feared "Country Club," which was the first private course I ever played. Apparently country-club golf was for me, as I ran away from my competition over the course of 17 holes. Then I got to the last hole. I pulled my drive left off of the tee, and my heart rate went up. I was thinking, "Just hang in there. Play for par or bogey, and go get your trophy." My next shot or two also stayed left. As I walked up to where my ball was supposed to be, there was a pond. I was devastated. I had no idea it was there. Per the rules, I dropped a new ball behind the pond and continued on. I hacked away all the way to the green while my playing partners paid no attention to me. They were well out of the running by then. After dropping my final putt, one of them asked me for my score. I said "8" and they said, "Wow, what happened?" I sullenly said, "I hit one in the drink."

As we walked to the clubhouse, I realized I really had a "9" but had signed my card for an "8." For you non-golfers, you must sign your scorecard after play to verify the correct score. If you sign for a number higher than your score, you are OK. If you sign for one lower than your score (in other words, a better score) you are disqualified. I went in the clubhouse completely torn. I then saw the leaderboard for my division and saw I was three shots clear of the field anyway. In my mind I rationalized it by saying, "Oh well, who cares if I won by two or three shots, I still won." But I didn't. I signed for a lower score. I should have been disqualified, but I didn't open my mouth. I walked up to the podium and accepted my token of victory: a wooden clock. Nearly 20 years later I still think about it, and the clock itself is still down in my basement. I'd like to give it back. If anyone who ran that tournament back in 1993 is reading this, shoot me an email. I have a clock I'd like to return . . . woo, I feel better now. Damn you, Matt Damon's character in "Bagger Vance" . . . or thank you I guess.

10

Bumper Stickers I'd Like to See

- I don't care who your dad is, unless your name is Jesus.
- Rectum? Damn near killed 'em.
- My other car is also a car.
- If you can read this, look up.
- Pittsburgh Steelers: Ten-time Super Bowl Champions
- Screw You, Carlos Boozer . . . 2011 Update: Screw You, LeBron James
- And You, Too, Webster Slaughter. I Hated Respecting You. (That's an obscure reference for you fans of the Steelers/Browns rivalry in the 1980s.)
- Tweet this.

And my favorite bumper sticker that I've seen on someone else's car: "Jesus is Coming. Look Busy."

11

More Travel Stories . . .

Bitten at LaGuardia Airport . . . Literally

Yesterday, I was sitting in LaGuardia waiting patiently for my delayed flight to get un-delayed back to Akron. A few gates down, I saw a small dog on a leash. That's an important point: on a leash, not in a cage. It was a Shih Tzu or a cute rat. Anyway, I love dogs so on my way back from the restroom, I was happy to see the little fella wander out in the aisle. Its little face just screamed "pet me." I think you see where this is going. As I reached down with my "hey little fella" dog voice, the evil gremlin tried to tear my hand off. It let out a vicious bark that drew looks from everyone in the Gate B area, as it made its attempt to make me its next victim. I pulled my hand from the clutches of certain death just in time, but not soon enough to catch a couple of teeth on my index finger.

The owner watched this happen, looked at the blood beginning to run from my hand and said "Kids, get the dog." Kids, get the dog? How about, "I'm sorry sir that you tried to be friendly and were nearly torn to shreds by this unruly hound." Or perhaps a warning that Killer is hungry and hates short, sarcastic people. Whatever. Anyway, if that wasn't embarrassing enough, I then had to turn around and walk back through that gate area to go to the bathroom to wash off the blood from the furry vampire's damage. People pointed . . . others whispered. In the end, I'm sure I've joined an extremely small club of people who can say they are dumb enough to be bitten by a dog at the airport. The problem is that the rest of this club's members are drug smugglers.

Driving Like Indy . . . I Mean to Indy

I was in Indianapolis Wednesday night and Thursday. I drove over from Ohio, so it was a solid five-hour drive one way. During that time, I observed a lot of things, such as the store sign that read "Karate, Guns and Tanning." I was by myself, so 10 hours is a long time for me to be trapped with my own thoughts. Here are some other observations from the trip:

1. It's amazing how you can remember song lyrics from 20 years ago but can't remember what you ate for dinner last night. Since no one was around, I was singing "Still of the Night" from the '80s hair band Whitesnake at the top of my lungs. Passing motorists were not impressed. The road can make you do crazy things.
2. Many people don't check their blind spots before changing lanes. About 12 times I saw the "oh shit" swerve move, where someone started to switch to an "occupied" lane. The other motorist usually honked

or told the merging driver that he or she was No. 1 through an animated gesture.

3. I confirmed the TV DVR has eliminated my ability to handle commercials. I hit the "Seek" radio button more times than I could count, trying to avoid commercials. (I know you can hit "Scan," but even four seconds of country music is too much for me. Sorry country fans.)

4. There is nothing between Columbus, Ohio and Indy. Seriously, Dayton is somewhere in there, but that stretch of I-70 is flat and straight. I could have driven without using my hands.

And finally . . . for some reason my rental car (a Mazda 6) had an exclamation point light up on the dash. I thought it was commending my singing or a sweet, Dale Earnhardt-like move to pass a truck. If you drive one, let me know if you've seen that before. I'm guessing it wasn't good.

The Ground Sounds Good About Now

This week's travels took me to San Diego on Tuesday and to Atlanta today. I once again had some adventures with the friendly skies. I had to fly through Atlanta to get to San Diego, and my track record through Atlanta is not good for on-time travel. I thought I had successfully made it through ATL without an issue yesterday, as we took off on time. About 15 minutes into the flight, the pilot comes on and says, "This is your captain. We are having a problem with one of the engines, so we are going to head back to Atlanta. But don't worry, everything is OK up here."

I'm glad all was well up front because those of us in the back who enjoy fully functional engines on our airplanes weren't as happy. Anyway, it all worked out. We had to get another plane, and we ended up being three hours late. Oh well. Definitely a time when "better late than never" was an appropriate description. On my return tonight, I figured I was good since I was staying in Atlanta for the night. The pilot announced, "We are on our final descent," and everything looked good as we headed toward the airport. As I looked out the window over the wing, I felt the plane quickly shift and pull back up . . . way up. The pilot then announced, "Sorry about that folks . . . nothing I could do there. Just a problem with traffic control. No mechanical issues." He sounded irritated. It reminded me of when I'd go on vacation with my family as a kid and my dad would be ticked off over missing a highway exit. The only difference was this was a plane, and the "exit" was the ground. In both cases, I was extremely uncomfortable. But anyway, we made a victory lap and eventually got to the ground. I've never been happier to see Baggage Claim.

12

"The Swings Begin"—
My Story, Part 3

If we rewind the story, I had my first bout of depression during my junior year of high school, but was not diagnosed as being bipolar. When I came out the other side, my energy was seemingly endless—and there was an edge to me that wasn't there before. By February of my junior year, things were getting back to normal. Sure I talked fast and seemed a bit more hyper than usual, but mostly everyone was just happy to see me off of the couch and enjoying life again.

Unfortunately the pendulum swung again that summer and, by August, I felt depressed again. I didn't know what to do. I was scared and confused and couldn't bear to think about feeling that way again. I tried to hide it for a while and started golf season, but I just couldn't get my mind right. So on a morning when I was supposed to be getting my senior pictures taken and going to a golf match, I told my mom I wasn't going to school again. Back to the doctor I went, but no hospitals came this time around. Instead the doctors let me stay home and get tutored. (I would like to thank the guy, Rich S., who tutored me. Although I knew him for quite a while because we both played basketball, it was awkward. He was cool though, despite the circumstances. I was just extremely embarrassed.)

The next three months were pretty uneventful, extremely frustrating and saddening for my family and friends. I rarely left the house. In fact I rarely left the couch. That same girlfriend stuck with me through it, even though she had to deal with people asking what was wrong with me and why I wasn't at school. She also missed things like the homecoming dance since I obviously wouldn't go.

But by late November, things began swinging the other way again. I eventually did go back to school, which surprised everyone. But again, I wasn't quite my old self. I talked fast, was disrespectful at times and was scattered. I tried to get back on the basketball team for the second half of the season, but the coach didn't think it was a good idea as he said he wanted to "get the younger guys some time." That just enraged me further. I always wanted to play varsity basketball and had worked throughout my childhood to overcome my height (I was 5 feet even my freshman year). I missed my junior year of basketball due to depression, and now I officially had no chance to ever play a minute of varsity.

I spent the last few months of my senior year doing whatever I felt like doing. Looking back I felt bad for taking advantage of teachers and friends who were giving me leeway as they'd rather have me in this somewhat-manic state than depressed and back at home. (One blessing is that I did not turn to illegal drugs any time I went on a manic run, which is pretty common for people battling this disease.)

I did graduate and closed my high school career with all A's and one C. That was in English, which was one of my best classes and was taught by my favorite teacher. When I questioned the grade, the teacher said I missed the participation points from not being in class. My mom asked me if I wanted her to protest this since I wouldn't be a valedictorian now. I asked her not to and chalked it up to a life lesson learned. If you don't show up, you can't get the prize. I had already been accepted to the honors program of a local college, so what was the difference?

13

"And the Pendulum Swings . . ."— My Story, Part 4

Again I went into the summer with things seemingly back to normal. But once again as August rolled around and college was around the corner, the old, crushing feelings came back. I tried to just keep working, bussing tables and washing dishes, hoping I'd pull out of it, but I couldn't. And when the day came when I was supposed to leave for college, I once again told my mom I couldn't do it. I called my friend from high school to tell him I was really sorry but wouldn't be joining him as his roommate. I then went back to bed, wondering if this was my curse for the rest of my life.

I laid around in a depressed funk for another three months. My parents' frustration grew by the day, but more importantly, they just wanted me to be OK. My girlfriend was now my ex-girlfriend, as she still had two more years of high school to enjoy. That crushed me even more. But I couldn't blame her. I couldn't see how anybody would want to be around me.

By December I was feeling better and got a job in the stock room of a local department store. And in January I started taking classes at a local university and was hanging out with friends again. But then the swing came again.

The energy was back at full tilt. I didn't sleep much but found that there was always someone to talk to on the Internet. (This was back when chatting first started in the mid-'90s, so America Online was gaining popularity very quickly.)

I began chatting regularly with a girl in Pennsylvania. She was about my age, and I enjoyed talking to her online. Eventually I got her phone number, and we started chatting by phone. My parents weren't real happy that I was blindly talking to someone, not to mention it wasn't cheap to chat or talk on the phone to someone in another state.

It didn't take much to push me into snap decisions, so I decided if my parents didn't like how I was acting, I would just leave. So I packed up my stuff and started driving. I called the girl from the chat room and said I was on the way to meet her in person. And I did. It was a seven-hour drive one way, but with my energy, that didn't seem so bad.

That kicked off a horrible run for me. I would pick up to drive to the girl's house whenever I felt like it. Driving all those hours with little to no sleep was not good. My parents tried to stop me but I did it anyway. They were afraid I was going to get hurt or at least get in trouble through my actions, and they were right.

On one trip home from the girl's house, I fell asleep behind the wheel and ended up in a snow bank in the median. Unbelievably I was safe, and no one was hurt. On another occasion, I was being tailgated by an angry truck driver. (I at least think he was angry.) I veered onto an off ramp to make my escape only to be going too fast to negotiate a turn and plowed into another snow drift. This time some guys (we'll call them some country fellas) gave me a ride to a gas station. The problem was they didn't have room in their truck so I had to ride in the back. It was probably 20 degrees so yes, it was chilly back there.

On that occasion, since I wasn't far from my girlfriend's house, I actually hitchhiked back there with a semi-truck driver. I approached him at the gas station and asked if he was going my way. When I hopped in, he could tell I was exhausted and told me I could lie down in the sleeper bunk if I wanted. I instantly thought, "Yeah right, I'm not into that." But eventually I got so tired that I did go back to the bunk as he drove. I had slipped a screwdriver under my sleeve just in case he tried any funny business, and I acted like I had gone to the sleep. He got on his phone as I listened intently. He actually called his wife, explained that he was giving me a ride and may be a little late. I decided that was enough proof that he was just doing me a favor, and I drifted off. He dropped me off at the girl's house and another tragedy was avoided. I caught a bus back to my car the next day, paid for the repairs and continued my "ride."

I quickly moved back to my parents' home. To try and appease me, they let me move down to the basement to have my own space. One night as the manic energy was rushing I decided to do some painting. In fact, I painted the entire basement—walls, floors, everything. The next morning my parents came down and saw my work. They were shocked, and I'm guessing not sure what to do next.

My stay was short-lived as I decided to move back out to live with a guy I knew from high school. I was still working at the department store, and one night I convinced a buddy from work named Rob to make the long drive with me over to see the girl in Pennsylvania. We drove through the night only to run out of gas at about 3:30 a.m. Luckily, a young woman stopped and gave us a ride to get gas—and we were back on our way. Through it all, it seemed like someone was always looking out for me, especially hitchhiking with that truck driver. This was just another example.

Anyway, after the all-night adventure I visited the girl for all of about three hours—and Rob and I were back on the road. Coming home I drove up a hill in Pennsylvania as rain came down. As I started down the hill, the rain had become ice. I lost control of the car (a 1989 Daytona) and weaved back and forth across the highway. Rob told me to take the car into the bank on the side of the road. I did what he said, but I hit the bank with the side of the car and it rolled over onto the roof. Unbelievably Rob and I only received some scrapes from the accident and a potential disaster was somewhat avoided.

From there, my behavior continued to be unruly at best. I got the car back to Ohio only to have the insurance company total it, but that didn't stop me. I decided I'd ride the bus from Ohio to Pennsylvania. And I did. That turned a usual seven-hour car ride into a 16-hour bus ride.

Even in the midst of the whirlwind that was my thinking, my old caring, compassionate self was still in there. I had to stop at a bus stop somewhere in Pennsylvania to switch to another bus. As I waited inside, I saw a large black man sitting by himself with a scowl on his face, nearly in tears. (I'm a short, white guy. Nothing racist here, just trying to paint the picture.) Anyway, I sat down beside him and said, "What's wrong with you?" The man just stared at me. I repeated, "Seriously, what's wrong with you?" The man was not nice as he said he needed five or 10 dollars to buy a ticket to get home. I can't remember how much exactly, only that it wasn't a huge amount.

I pulled out what I had left in my wallet and said, "Here." The man couldn't believe I was willing to help him so quickly. He thanked me and went off to buy his ticket.

I then went on to start up a chat with a young lady with a small child. I love kids and started entertaining the kid as we waited. The child laughed, and I took off my hat to put it on the child's head as we played. "Oh don't do that," the lady said. He doesn't like anything on his head." I put the hat on him anyway and said the kid would look good in a Steelers hat. The child just smiled and sat with the hat on. The lady said, "I've never seen him wear a hat like that before." I just smiled and said, "Keep it." I then went to find a pay phone to see if my parents could wire me some money. The ride continued . . . .

When I got back from the bus trip, my parents knew they had to act fast to try and get me under control. My dad challenged me about selling my college books to gain some quick cash. I had sold a couple of them, but not all of them and promptly went upstairs to pull out the books I had. I then promptly threw them against the wall. My dad came toward me, and I pulled the dresser over in front of him. That was the last straw, and my parents called the police.

I was led out of the house and took the ride to the police station. I wasn't charged with anything, but no one really wanted to come and help me either. (Actually they did, but I didn't think that was the case.) So the police dropped me off at a halfway house for the night and told my parents where I was. That was one of the lowest points in my life. All I could think was how could I be there? This place was for homeless people or those addicted to drugs, not for me. Don't get me wrong, in my manic state I still talked to everyone I could and joked around, but I still couldn't believe where I was.

My parents called and said I could come home, but I'd have to go to the hospital first. I took their offer and went quietly to the hospital. I received treatment over a few days to calm me down and eventually went back home to my parents, feeling somewhat normal again. I got another car and still visited the girl in Pennsylvania. That excitement soon ran out, and I broke it off. I was working again at a grocery store and was back in school in September, and the grades were coming easy to me again. But the ride wasn't over yet.

14

"I Ride On . . . and Crash"—
My Story, Part 5

The funny thing about being bipolar is just how damn unpredictable it is . . . yes, I say that in jest, but it's also the truth. Returning to the story, as I said I was back in college and doing well in the fall semester. Unfortunately it wasn't long before the mania came back for another round.

I can't pinpoint when the transition began. If I could have, there wouldn't be so many colorful stories about my antics. Anyway, by the time late fall rolled around, the Ward Express was rolling again. I was pulling straight A's at school but my thoughts were racing once again. I didn't need much sleep, and my confidence was extremely high.

I had the answer for everything. When challenged about religion I told a classmate, "God helps me when I need him, and he let's me handle it the rest of the time." My classmate disagreed, but I wouldn't hear it. I knew better than she did. I was also in the habit of writing bad checks, which my dad eventually cleaned up for me.

Days and nights began to blur together. One night I had a 10-page paper to write for my college English class. I waited until 1 a.m. the day it was due to start it and wrote it though the night. My dad came down to go to work to find me finishing the paper. He was upset that I was staying up all night. He knew something wasn't right, but trying to get through to me was impossible. And what did I write about? I wrote a paper on how I disagreed with Albert Einstein on a variety of topics. I think the overconfidence was showing through. For what's it's worth, I did get a "B" on the paper—but the professor cited that I failed to have solid proof to back up my arguments. Sounds about right.

I continued rolling at a thousand miles an hour, and my thoughts were becoming more and more bizarre. I began to feel like "evil" or the devil was trying to get me. One night while driving home from a concert, my friend asked if he could drive my truck—a five-speed, standard pickup truck. I agreed and pulled off the side of the highway. As my friend went to pull out on the highway, he was struggling with the stick shift—and we were nearly struck by another vehicle that came up quickly behind him. I was sure that the devil or some evil force was trying to attack us. My friend didn't lead on at the time, but inside I'm sure he was scared to death.

You can only go so long on a manic run like this. Convinced that I couldn't live at home anymore I grabbed my things again and moved out. After staying at a low-budget motel for a night, I reported in to work at the grocery store. I told people there that I was heading to New York to start a new life. One of the girls I worked with pleaded with me to stay. In my state, I jumped to the conclusion that this girl wanted to be with me (despite her large, angry boyfriend) so I agreed to stay.

I checked into another hotel. This time it was a much nicer, new hotel. I was still barely sleeping but did make it to some of my college exams. I blew through a test in a class called "Seven Ideas That Shook the Universe" and walked out of the room before many were nowhere close to finished. Unfortunately (or fortunately) I hit the wall before I could complete all of my exams. I wasn't eating or sleeping right so I was losing weight quickly, as classmates had even noticed my pants hanging off of me. They didn't know about my evening activities.

At night at the hotel, I swam lap after lap in the pool. I was never that good of a swimmer, but I felt like I was now great at it. I would then jump out of the pool and dribble a basketball around the outside of the pool weaving in and out of chairs. Then I'd dive back in and go back to the swimming. I was convinced that I was going to live my dream of playing basketball since I missed out in high school. This time I planned to play at a small college where an older player I admired from high school had attended and played. Unfortunately that guy had been killed in a car accident, and I felt he was there with me in the pool pushing me to train to meet my goals. I was basically on the brink of breaking down completely.

Over the course of a few nights I had friends visit me at the hotel, and I freaked them out with my stories and delusions of grandeur. I began recording my thoughts on a tape recorder as I thought my racing thoughts about the world might make a good book one day. I still felt something evil was messing with me and trying to stop me from making the world a better place. Like I said, delusions of grandeur.

Finally the end came. I went back to the pool on my last night at the hotel and began swimming. The next thing I knew, I woke up in the pool. I still don't know what happened. I may have passed out or just fallen asleep on the side of the pool. Maybe got a little wake-up call from above. Who knows?

All I did know was that I needed to call my parents and go home. I was instantly excited that this was so clear to me now. I ran back to my room and called my mom and asked if I could come home. She said of course but I'd have to get help first. I agreed but simply was gone by then. I hung up and started flinging all of my belongings that I had in the room into the hallway. I then began dribbling my basketball and running up and down the hallway as fast as I could. I would stop momentarily to look at the line of the traffic out the window that I thought was coming to glorify me as some type of second coming-like figure. The hotel staff called the police, but luckily my parents got there at the same time. They called the hospital, and an ambulance was called to get me.

My parents took to removing my things from the hotel while also apologizing to the hotel staff and police for tolerating my behavior. Meanwhile I began the ride north in the ambulance. I actually recognized one of the staff members in the ambulance as he used to play basketball at another local high school. At the time I thought it was great to see him. I still see him occasionally today and honestly try to avoid him. To say the least, I was embarrassed by our last encounter.

Anyway, the ambulance staff tried to get me calmed down with a sedative, but my arms were too tense to take the needle. I was totally amped on adrenaline and a complete manic eruption.

When I got to the emergency room, I was placed in a room while waiting to be formally admitted and transported eventually to the psychiatric ward. I was still hallucinating and was positive that Eddie Murphy (yes, the comedian and actor) was out in the hallway and was obviously there to tell me how great I was. I started yelling, "I know you! I know you, Eddie!" which was a line from one of Murphy's stand-up routines. After that, I noticed my knee was bleeding from slamming it into a chair at the pool. Instead of calling for a nurse, I saw a roll of gauze in the room and started wrapping it up myself. A nurse came in to confront me, and I told her to calm down as I could handle it!

Looking back I laugh at this story, but I'm also alarmed by it. How could I think this way? The scarier part is how I can remember it like I was a bystander outside of my own body watching it happen. Mania is a crazy thing. You can remember basically everything that you do, even if your friends and family don't want to think you can remember it. In mania, I was always right. Everyone else was wrong. I thought I was thinking at a higher level than everyone else. I was enlightened. It was my job to get others to see what I was seeing. Unfortunately I couldn't see what I had become.

15

"The Diagnosis"— My Story, Part 6

I spent the next week in the hospital. The first few days were rough as I continued to "come down." I was strapped down to my bed on one occasion. I determined I'd show the staff a thing or two and proved I could wiggle my way to get my head down to where my feet were. I then screamed at them out the door to show them what I had accomplished. On another day, my brother and his wife came to visit me. Since there was a surveillance camera back in the visiting area, I decided to show off and "moon" the camera to show off for my brother. It was funny right up until a nurse came in with a needle and shot a sedative in my ass. My mooning days were done. (You would think I would have learned from years of getting in trouble from showing off for my brother, but old habits die hard!)

Eventually I slowed down and spent my days channeling my energy into doing sit-ups and shooting pool. I will never forget one particular day when a large man who was also being treated in the ward was watching me bounce around the room. As I sat down on the couch, the man approached me. I thought he was going to tell me to settle my ass down or even physically attack me. But instead the man grasped my head and said a prayer for me. It calmed me down a bit and from then on, things seemed to smooth out.

Not surprisingly I was finally officially diagnosed with bipolar depression and placed on lithium. I was soon released back to my parents to try and get my life back together. I got back to school in the spring semester and found the medication was working. By August I was packing to head to college an hour from home to start taking on life without Mom and Dad. I'm happy to say that the treatment worked, and I went on to get my degree without issue. In fact, three years later I thought I had defied the odds and went off of my medication. It is well-known that this is a regular mistake by bipolar patients when they start feeling better. Amazingly I maintained a regular life for the next 12 years. Looking back, I think I was riding the bipolar wave during that time, but I was just able to keep it in check. But as you'll read later, manic depression can lie dormant—but it's usually not dead. And of course, I'll tell you how I'm proof of that.

16

One House, Two Houses . . .
One Mouse, Two Mice?

Like I said earlier, I'm a communications dork. A word weenie if you will. With that said, I have some bones to pick with the English language. If you are trying to learn English as a second language, there are just some things that don't make sense to me, so I'm guessing they can't make much sense for you. Here are some examples:

- I have a house. If I get another, I have two houses. Logic says if I see a mouse and then another, I'd see two mouses. Oh no. You've seen two mice. But wait, does that mean, I also own two hice? Nope. You have two houses, and you've seen two mice.
- OK that's fine, but what if I see a moose and then another. I've seen two mooses, right? No. You've seen two moose. No need to add the "s." Got it? Alright then, so if I have a goose and then get another, I have

two goose right? Of course not, you have two geese. Really? So why didn't I see two meese then?

- You put your foot in a boot, but they don't make the same sound.
- I read the book, and that apple is red. "Read" rhymes with "red" when it's in the past tense, but "read" rhymes with "reed" in the present tense. That's easy, right?
- Back to that boot. If there are two of them I have a pair of boots, right? YES! So I put my foots in my boots? NO. Oh so I put my feet in my beet? No. You eat a beet, or you can beat an egg. You could even beat a beet with your feet.

Forget it. Habla Espanol?

17

"The Relapse"—
My Story, Part 7

After nearly 12 years of managing bipolar on my own, without medication, I assumed I had beaten my enemy. In fact, I was sure of it. I had a good job, a great wife, a new house—and life seemed to be pretty good. Little did I know, the big D (depression) was creeping back into my life. In February 2009, I felt a bit sluggish—but the Steelers winning the Super Bowl helped propel me through that month. I'm a big Steelers fan, so yes, I'm that excited when they win a big game.

By April, stress was wearing on me. I had to let someone go at work while my company went through a layoff. I now had two mortgages, and my renters were moving out of my old place. I felt the old feelings of depression coming back, and it scared me to death. My wife had never seen this side of me. Would she think I was crazy? I didn't feel like she signed up for this shit . . . even if she was to love "for better or worse." I got help in May and battled my way through the worst summer I ever had (to that point). But this time, I didn't shut it down. I kept getting up in the morning. I kept going to work. I took up running. I kept lifting weights. I tried to fight this time, and I'm proud to say I came out the other side by the end of the summer. I felt like I owed my wife a better explanation than I could verbalize, so I wrote an essay for her and for others who battle similar demons. The following is what I wrote for my wife and also to potentially share with others who were suffering. Unfortunately what I didn't know is that when I wrote this, I was heading toward mania again.

You Can Always Score a Knockout in the 10th . . .

It happens every year. As we head into another holiday season and the days get shorter and the weather gets colder, something else happens. More people suffer from depression. I'm not going to get into seasonal affective disorder, as that's a topic in itself. I'd like to discuss my experience with depression, fights and rematches I've had with it, and most importantly how if you've stepped in the ring with it, you aren't alone.

If you suffer from depression, it can occur at any time. My most recent bout with it just came over the spring and summer. Unfortunately this is my favorite time of the year. I love to be outside, play golf, go to the beach or just sit outside and enjoy a beer. When you are depressed, the enjoyment just isn't there. In my case, snow and cold have nothing to do it. Something occurring physiologically does. I guess it has something to do with chemical imbalances or something like that. I can't explain it, as I haven't felt that way in about 10 years. But for those this may help, I'll try to tell you about my experiences so you know if you are gripped by this, you aren't alone and things will get better.

When I'm depressed, I enjoy nothing. The days become a routine of waking up, hoping it's not time to get out of bed and then being overcome by fear when it is time I know I have to get going. As I lay there, my mind has a tendency to race, mostly with negative thoughts and worries about things that, in reality, will most likely never come to fruition. And if my mind doesn't go there, I start to think of all the things I've regretted doing in my past. I start feeling like I'm a bad person and maybe everything I usually stand for, like hard work and putting others' needs ahead of my own, is just a façade. I know . . . pretty heavy stuff for 7 a.m. When I was younger and suffering my depression, my parents did whatever they could to help me—including giving me the escape of not going to school after unsuccessfully trying to coerce me to go didn't work. Now as an adult, I know that isn't an option anymore. If I didn't have the parents I have, I would have probably been out on the streets when I was 18. But again, that's a story for another day.

So once I do make it out of bed, everything becomes a laborious chore. Work seems insurmountable. Trivial tasks like taking out the trash become events to worry about. It's a struggle to do just about anything. I watch the clock, almost obsessively, thinking about how I'm wasting the day and wasting my life. I try to concentrate, but the Big D just won't let me. (The Big D is depression, not some monster or contagious condition.) Trying to talk to others is even worse. It's tough to put thoughts together. I talk slower, stop in the middle of thoughts often and probably make a lot of people uncomfortable, especially when they are used to dealing with me and used to having trouble getting a word in over my usual fast-paced banter.

Things I usually enjoy, like playing basketball or video games or just hanging out with family and friends, become things to avoid. I just try to make it through the day with as little interaction with others as possible. Why? Because what if they keep prying about what's wrong with me? What if they ask me to do something I don't want to do? What if they find out I'm dealing with the Big D? It sounds ridiculous now, but when you are in it and the Big D is winning every round, all you want to do is throw in the towel. Going to bed seems like the only escape, as each day crawls on at a snail's pace. But for me, even sleep does not come easily when the Big D's around.

Sounds fun, huh? Well it's not. And if you've ever dealt with depression over a prolonged period of time, you know what it's like. Those who haven't, simply don't know. They can read about it, ask for advice and try to help. But they simply can't wear your shoes. All they can do is cheer from the crowd. Even worse, when you feel that way, you wonder how everyone else is having such a damn good time around you. Sure they notice you aren't acting the same, but they go ahead and carry on with their lives. And there you are, left standing in the middle of the ring with the Big D staring at you, angry as a bull and ready to knock your head off. And no matter what you do, you just can't seem to land a punch.

OK, so I may be taking this boxing analogy a bit far, but I'm a sports fanatic so cut me a break. Anyway, that's just a snapshot of how I feel when I'm depressed. When I'm in it, I feel like there is no way out, and it's never going to end. But this time around, I did some things to keep myself in the fight. Because I know now, if I can keep standing, keep moving forward, take my pounding and not quit, I'll still be standing there in the 10th round. And the Big D will be standing there as well, shaking its head like Apollo Creed when Rocky picks himself off the mat and asks for more after taking a horrendous beating. (That's a great scene, by the way. One of the greatest in movie history in my opinion.) Again, that's a conversation for another day.

So what did I do this time? It begins with self-awareness and recognition of the problem. I didn't deny it this time around. I've been here before. The first thing I did is talk to my family. As much as it pained me to talk to them about it, I did. My wife, my mom, my brother and sister, my father—all of them. I tried to tell them how I was feeling. Of course, I relayed my feelings of hopelessness and how I didn't know if I'd feel better this time around. But they stayed in my corner, offered their encouragement and kept telling me to stay in there and fight. Support from others is big, even when you can't see it at the time.

What else did I do? I took their advice. I got help. I went to my family doctor. He put me on an antidepressant. I reluctantly agreed. After two weeks, I went back to him saying how it wasn't working. He tweaked the dosage and sent me back out there. He also offered the help of a psychologist or psychiatrist. This time around I did not go that route, as I've been there before as well. But don't get me wrong, that is definitely a good route to go. I actually called a psychiatrist my doctor recommended. Coincidentally my mother recommended the same guy. Unfortunately he wasn't covered by my insurance, and I didn't pursue it any further. With that said, if you are depressed, it is definitely a smart thing to do. There is no shame in it. It's a small price to pay for happiness.

But back to the fight. I tried to stay active whenever I had the energy to do so. I forced myself to keep going to the gym and lift weights. I felt like I had nothing to give and it was useless, but I told myself to keep doing it. For brief moments as I focused on lifting, I could forget about the fight. In fact, I was actually landing some punches finally and didn't even realize it. It felt good to sweat. Basketball was out as I simply did not want the interaction with the other guys I've been playing with for years. They wouldn't understand, and my ridiculously slow reaction time would make it even more obvious I was having issues. But lifting weights, I was on my own. I could lift, ride the stationary bike, do some sit-ups . . . anything to keep the blood going. My interactions were limited to head nods and simple hellos to acquaintances I usually see in there. It was the perfect recipe for me.

What else? I forced myself to get out of the house when I could. I went on walks with my wife. She obliged, even though I didn't say much if anything at all. I started to jog. First a half mile, then eventually one mile, then two. I played golf with my brother and friends when they asked me. I never took the initiative to ask them but, when they asked me, I went. I wasn't myself, but the competitive side of me began creeping back to life.

I started planning on doing things outside of today or tomorrow. I agreed to go on vacation with my family, even though I feared I wouldn't feel better when vacation time rolled around. It worked out great. Being with family at the place I enjoyed the most—the beach—really helped me start to get out of my funk.

I also kept doing what I had to do at work. I knew I wasn't performing at my best, but that didn't mean others had to know it. I kept going, kept showing up at meetings—still didn't say much, but I was there. As the days went on, this got easier. My confidence began to return slowly but surely, and most people (outside of those closest to me at work) were none the wiser.

But most importantly, I did not give up this time. Although I wanted to throw in the towel every day for nearly three months, I didn't. I couldn't. I felt like the most selfish person in the world during this time. But at the times when I knew I would let someone down I cared about, I did what I had to do to keep going. Little things go a long way, especially when you are dealing with the ones you love most.

So here I sit today. I wrote this article in the time it took my wife to get her eyebrows waxed. That's right. She just called me a half hour ago and said she was stopping to do that on her way home, so I thought I'd pass some time and share my story. The cold is setting in and the holidays are around the corner, and I feel better than ever. I'm back to top form at work, I'm playing basketball three or four times a week and I'm enjoying life . . . every damn minute of it. I even stopped by the doctor last week to tell him I'm back, and we should start to lower my dosage of Effexor and prepare to get me off it. His response was, "Nice idea, but let's get you through the winter when depression is the most common. Come see me in January, and we'll talk then." I agreed. That also gave me the idea to write this article.

I hope if you are reading this that it can be of some help to you. If you are fighting the Big D right now, you may be thinking, "Good for you tough guy. Now leave me alone. You don't know how it feels!" But that's just it. I do. And so do thousands of other people. You aren't alone. You can beat it if you want to. Sure the Big D looks like Ivan Drago in Rocky IV. I get it. But if you keep getting off the mat, keep listening to your corner (your family, friends and medical professionals) and refuse to throw in the towel, you can make it to that last round . . . and knock the Big D out. He'll never see it coming.

18

Gun Control

I've already touched on religion as a topic so why not move on to another one that creates heated debate: gun control. I just don't get it. So let me paint my ideal scenario for you and then try to address some of the issues I know the pro-gun people will have with my thoughts.

Let's make all guns illegal—all of them, everywhere, with some exceptions that I'll get to in a minute. Some of you are intrigued; others are calling me four-letter words and a tree hugger. The bottom line is people couldn't get killed by guns if they weren't around.

In the first phase of my plan, only police officers and members of the military would be authorized to carry guns. If they misused guns in any way, they would be relieved of their duties or dealt with by the law if necessary. No one else can have one. That's it.

Let me get to those counterpoints now.

#1. The Bill of Rights Argument

The easy argument is to point to our constitutional right "to bear arms." But come on people. Don't you think things have changed a little in the 250 years since this made sense? The last time I checked, most of us don't need to worry about a bear wandering into our yard—and I'm not too concerned about British soldiers trying to ransack my home. It was a different time. Back in the day of our forefathers trying to establish that freedom thing and defending their land, I could see why people had the right to bear arms. I don't think the spirit of the bill was to protect drug dealers who may want to use a gun to kill someone or intimidate others. I don't think the intention was for street gangs to have them to drive by and shoot rival gang members. I think it's simple. Yes, you can say I am taking up an argument against our Bill of Rights. But I think if those who wrote it could see how things are today, they'd have an issue too.

#2. I'm a Hunter

I am not a hunter, but I can appreciate that many people enjoy doing it. I'm not a fan of doing it for sport, but hey, that's another debate altogether. I do understand that in some areas you must keep the deer population under control or it creates unsafe situations for both people and the animals. With that said, we could have hunters sign up to hunt. This already exists at hunting resorts all over the world where you can rent equipment. I'd like to extend that to everywhere. Hunters can travel to whatever areas are in need of thinning herds and have at it. When they arrive, they can "rent" a gun and check it in and out each day. At the end of their trip, they go home—and the gun stays under lock and key at the appropriate facility. I think that's reasonable. If you only have guns to hunt, why do you need them at home?

#3. Protection

There are good people who have guns to protect themselves from the bad people who have guns. If we can get the guns away from both parties, I'm guessing deaths and murders would go down around the world. But of course, that's just my opinion. The bottom line is there are people with good intentions and bad intentions everywhere in the world. Maybe if you made it harder for those with bad intentions to get weapons or other tools to help them wreak havoc, we would be better off. Today, we have conceal-and—carry laws. You can't tell the good people from the bad, so you definitely can't tell if someone with a gun has good intentions. If you took them away from everyone, it would be pretty easy to tell if there was going to be an issue. If someone had a gun (and wasn't a cop or soldier), you'd know he or she had it illegally. I'm guessing that means the person has bad intentions.

I won't take this one any further. I'm guessing that those of you who are card-carrying NRA members would like to see me step in front of you at a rifle range. Others may think I have a point here. Like I said, it's just my opinion.

19

I Hate Text Messaging

I hate text messaging on cellphones. This may be the most irritating thing ever created. Have you ever sat in the same room with someone having a text message conversation? Looking at the phone, thumb typing . . . looking away from the phone. A minute later the phone buzzes . . . look at the phone, decipher the message, thumb type, look away from the phone. Then repeat the process 20 times.

I'm guessing that a 15-minute text conversation equates to a one-minute phone call. If I'm using my phone to text and you are using the phone to text, how about we use our phones to talk to each other? I understand that sometimes texting comes in handy if you can't necessarily have a conversation. But my guess is that this is not the case in the majority of these situations. Some do it for the novelty. Others do it because they don't want to make the "commitment" to actually have a conversation. The text language is bothersome to me too. One, I can't speak it, nor do I want to. Call me crazy, but I like to see some vowels in the words I'm reading.

Also, I think texting is making our young people dumber. Many of them can't write a complete sentence, while others cringe at the idea of having a face-to-face conversation. You can't text your answers to a job interview folks . . . at least not yet.

So there you go. I feel better. Hw r u?

20

Please Put on a Towel . . . Please.

This really has no place in this book, but I guess you could say that about a lot of these chapters. I now turn my focus to the gym—more specifically, the locker room. Now I can only speak from a male's perspective on this, but this may be one of the more disturbing places for me to visit. Here are some tips I'd love to share with the guys I see at the local YMCA:

1. A towel can be used for more than drying off. In fact, you can be creative and use it to cover up as you make the long walk back from the shower.
2. If you insist on putting lotion on your legs, you don't need to hike your leg up on the bench for all to see your junk. Again, you can cover up with a towel and still put lotion on your legs. It's been done.

3. Treat it like your bathroom at home. I doubt you display the remains of your shaving experience as prominently on your sink at home. If you do, don't invite me over.
4. Wear shower shoes. This is more for your own good than mine.
5. Courtesy flush. Enough said here.

21

In Closing . . . (This was supposed to be the end.)

So that's it, folks. I hope you were able to take at least one thing away from this book that could help you or at least maybe something back there made you smile or laugh. Some days it feels like I've seen enough to know I've seen too much. (I stole that from "A League of Their Own.") Other days I feel like I don't know anything. At least I now know that there's plenty I don't know. You probably figured that out if you've made it this far in this collection of my ramblings.

Anyway, I think this life thing can be boiled down to some pretty simple principles. I'd like to say I came up with them, but I'll have to give the nod to God and Jesus on these ones. Treat people how you'd like to be treated. Be selfless, not selfish. Serve others, don't look to be served. Keep the faith and don't waver in the face of adversity. Simple, right? I know, easier said than done, which leads to "don't be a hypocrite."

Even with all that, things can get tough sometimes. As they say, everyone has their own crosses to bear. But you have to remember that the night is darkest before the dawn. (Someone else said that too.)

So I'll leave you with this. Try to enjoy every day, and don't take time for granted. Even when the worst things are going on in your life, try to find one good thing to raise your spirits. If you don't have faith in Jesus, focus on whatever it is you believe in.

And finally, remember to change things up. Say yes more than no. Try new foods. Travel to new places—even if it's in your own city or state. Don't be afraid to change things up occasionally. All routines are self-inflicted. Sometimes I grow a goatee just to change my look a bit, but also so I don't have to shave as much as I hate shaving every day. I then have fun with it as people always comment about my new look. Then when I'm goofing around and say something off-color, I blame it on my new "alter ego" who is donning the goatee. Hell, I even gave him a name. You can call me Ron.

22

But Wait, There's More

So that was supposed to be the big shocking ending to this one as you find out that I am actually "Ron." Anyway, it's probably a good thing I didn't call it a day and turn this in for publication. Why? Because there is obviously more story to tell here and also I didn't have enough words to actually get this thing published. How's that for honesty?

The funny thing is that I am now sitting here approximately 16 months after I originally began writing this thing. I went back and read some of what I've written, and it's easy to tell (at least for me) when I was a little (or a lot) manic while writing. If you go back and read the earlier chapters and think I sound preachy or arrogant or all-knowing, that's a pretty good signal I had some mania action working. In fact the only reason I found a self-publishing company, paid for its services and started writing this thing was due to the overly enhanced self-confidence I have when I'm on the high side of the bipolar road. So again if you go back to the intro of this book when I told my wife I was going to write a book, that was pretty much brought on by rolling in a manic state. Pretty cool, huh? That's a joke, of course.

Also, if you go back you'll find dated references to movies and other things. I was going to go back and change those too, but that's too tough to do and would compromise the facts in my story. You'll just have to understand that this book was written over a period of time. Here' how that timeline went:

- March 2010: Began frantically writing at all times of day and night.
- April/May 2010: Writing slowed as I returned to "normal" and then dipped back into depression.
- May/June: No writing.
- July: One entry written while hitting rock bottom on a trip to Florida for work (found in Chapter 24).
- July 2010-July 2011: No writing.
- July 2011: Writing again. In fact, today it is 11 p.m. July 12. The Major League All-Star game is on . . . .
- February-March 2012: Writing concludes.

So there you go. If my references are dated, so what? "The Hurt Locker" was still a great movie, and Justin Timberlake is still unfortunately on my iPod. Don't judge me. Now on with the show . . . .

23

"Riding the Waves Again"— My Story, Part 9

As you look at the timeline in Chapter 22, you can see by my writing activity when things went south. In the spring of 2010, I had a great time. I bought a new car. We joined a country club. I had a work trip take me to Puerto Rico in March, so I took my wife with me. We then went to Las Vegas for her spring break (she's a teacher) and then planned a trip to Myrtle Beach in June with my family. Yes, it was a lot of spending for me, but the manic side makes me a little "loose" with my money to say the least. Luckily we were in a financial situation that allowed us to absorb my spending. And my wife didn't think much of it as she was just glad that I was off of the couch and enjoying life again. The people at Home Depot also appreciated it when I swung by to browse and walked out with new deck furniture and a power washer. I have to admit that the power washer is pretty sweet though. After I got done cleaning the siding, I went ahead and blasted the sidewalks just for the fun of it. Totally awesome.

Anyway, the high petered out for good around April, and by May I was getting worried. I remember being in Los Angeles at a trade show and telling a co-worker that I just didn't feel right physically. I told my wife I was feeling lethargic. I'd been there before. The depression was coming, and once again I waited too long to stop it. I returned home with a sales meeting coming up the next week and a trip to Myrtle Beach following that. I made it through the sales meeting without bringing any attention to my condition. I followed up with my family physician to try and stop it, but the medication he recommended didn't get the job done. I tried to tell myself that if I could just make it to vacation, I could pump the drugs into my body and come back ready to go. I was wrong.

Vacation was not fun. I was with my wife, parents, my brother and his family. This usually would mean a great time as I love spending time with my family. My days were pretty much filled with sitting on the beach falling asleep off and on all day. I did try some self-medicating in the afternoon with a few cold beers. They did actually make me feel a little better as I temporarily forgot about being miserable, but that was short lived each day. It was sad that I looked forward to drinking beer each day as a pick-me-up.

After a week of worrying about returning home and to work, we started home. I remember each hour I drove thinking about how the hell I was going to able to function at work. My mind was constantly racing with negative thoughts. Everything felt like the end of the world. I couldn't cope with anything. At the same time I tried to hang in there as I didn't want to put my wife through this again.

I went back to work the following Monday, but I knew I couldn't do it much longer. I would sit and stare at my computer screen for stretches of time. I still did the work I needed to do, but it took me longer and everything slowed down. Even the time it took me to process what someone was telling me and then return a verbal response felt like it took forever. When you are a manager of "communications," that makes the job a little rough. By July 2010, I was at rock bottom again and wrote this:

So I figured it wasn't fair to only write about being depressed after you've come out of it. In fact, I went back and read what I wrote before and now I feel like a hypocrite.

I am in the middle of a bout with depression right now, and I'm struggling. I'm not proud of how I'm handling things this time around. I feel selfish as I put my self-pity above the needs of the people I care about. My thoughts are scattered and filled with hopelessness. You'll probably pick up on that as you read this. I try to fill time that I don't have to be at work by watching TV or at least staring at it. I watch the clock a lot, hoping it will slow down so I don't have to go to work or anywhere for that matter. That in itself is kind of funny as I'm writing this on a plane on my way to Florida for work. Go figure. That scares me as well as I'm just not myself. An even scarier thought is that maybe this is me.

Thinking back over the five or six months prior to this I'm pretty sure I had some manic action going. One night I stayed up until 2 or 3, went to bed, got back up at 4, did a yoga workout and then went and played basketball at 5. After that I went to work and then to a dinner. That's not right. Also over the past six months, I think we spent too much money. I won't go into the details, but it wasn't my usual conservative spending patterns.

This time I did go see a psychiatrist, and he changed up my medications a couple of days ago. Hopefully, I'll start to see some positive changes. Something has to give. I just hope the depression gives before I do.

I do have to give it to my wife. She puts up with me with a smile on her face. I'm glad we also got a dog a while back, as he's providing her with some needed playful companionship instead of only having her lump of a husband to be with. He also provides me with some moments where I forget about feeling sorry for myself as we play.

There's not much more to say. I hope I've hit bottom and am on the climb back up. I have a good wife, family and job. I don't want to screw that up. I also need to turn things over to Jesus.

24

Even Awards Suck—
My Story, Part 10

The one positive thing during that "down" time was a good friend at work actually got me in to see a psychiatrist. I had tried to manage this thing long enough with a family practitioner. Even he agreed that I needed a specialist. Little did I know at the time this was the beginning of my long-term solution.

In mid-July I was pretty much cooked. I remember on July 19 I laid in bed until almost noon. I was able to drag myself out in time to head into the office. My wife was in the bathroom doing her hair and she said, "Who knows, maybe this day will be better."

I went in to make sure my video guy was set up to tape an awards presentation. These awards were the most prestigious offered by my company. Our executives presented the winners one by one, as they were surprisingly joined by their loved ones to congratulate them. I was just happy to be out of that spotlight when to my surprise my vice president took the stage and announced me as a winner. I was horrified. I walked up to shake his hand while my wife came out to congratulate me as well. I took a couple of awkward pictures, accepted hugs and handshakes from my co-workers and did whatever I could to make it look like I was happy. I had worked extremely hard for the company over the past 11 years, but at that time I didn't feel like I was worthy of the award. I didn't feel worthy of anyone's praise for anything. I felt embarrassed to even be recognized even as people told me how well deserved it was.

The award came with a nice bonus check that I placed in a drawer at home. I told my wife I wasn't going to cash it as I didn't feel I deserved it. Her response was, "That's fine. Just cash it and give it to me!" Of course her comment was in jest, but I did go ahead and cash it. It sat in our savings account for more than a year. And on a related note, we eventually used it to pay for part of a trip to Jamaica. (I guess that's a spoiler alert I'm feeling better now as I'm writing this.)

25

"My Last Day"—
My Story, Part 11

My birthday is July 26. Once again on that day, I stayed in bed until nearly noon before going into the office. I received some "Happy Birthday" wishes from my team, but I was far from happy. It was terrible being there. I felt like I could contribute nothing.

The next morning I did not go in at all. My boss called and told me I should consider going on short-term disability until I figured out the medication. I was reluctant to accept the offer and tried to tell myself that I just needed a few more days to work myself out of this funk. By the next week, I was officially "off the clock." I must admit I felt a bit of relief that I would not have to deal with the "horror" of going to work at least for a little while. I soon found out that I was cleared to be out until the first week of September. Four weeks sounds like a good period of time to get back on your feet, but I just viewed it as an opportunity to buy some time before I'd have to take more drastic measures like quitting my job or even worse.

August totally sucked for me and possibly even more so for my poor wife. I rarely got out of bed before noon. I only got up long enough to go to the couch and crash again. I would watch SportsCenter and whatever else came on ESPN hour after hour. My wife would try and force me to go with her to walk the dog or just go to the store, but I fought her every step of the way. I did not want to be seen outside of the house. I had people ask me after the fact if I played golf or went swimming and hung out during that time. The answer was absolutely not. I made my house my own prison. I didn't leave it unless absolutely necessary. I occasionally would sit on my deck and stare at the sky, but that was the extent of it. My phone would ring with calls from my boss and my friends at work, but I never answered. I didn't want to talk to them. And even if I answered, I didn't know what to say. Once again I was embarrassed. I did check my email every once in a while just to see what was going on at work. I quickly learned that many of the emails I received really didn't need a response from me as I was just "copied" on the message. For fun, go and look at how many messages really need a response from you. I'm not talking about what you respond to but what truly warrants a response. You soon don't feel as important as you thought you were. The world simply moves on without you.

26

"Don't Call it a Comeback"— My Story, Part 12

OK so I just wanted to start with that title because I always liked the beginning of that LL Cool J song. I believe that was "Mama Said Knock You Out," but let's get back to the topic at hand.

So obviously if I'm making LL Cool J jokes I'm feeling pretty good once again. But in getting back to my story, I did go back to work. I decided to agree with my doctor that I should go back a week earlier than originally planned.

That Monday I stayed in bed and decided I'd try the next day. I was scared to death. How would people view me if I went back? Would they think I'm crazy? Would they treat me differently? I needed at least one more day to psych myself out of going.

When Tuesday rolled around I stayed in bed until about 9:30 a.m. and decided it was time to try. I went in the office. I stopped at my buddy's desk and answered a question like nothing had ever happened. He just said, "Good to see you, dude." Another girl who reports to me popped out of her cubicle and said how excited she was to see me. You could tell she couldn't decide if I'd be OK with a hug or not, so she just let me pass on to my office.

I kicked off my first hour in the office after a month by going to lunch with my friends in the department. I'd been gone 30 days, what would another hour hurt? We sat out on the patio, as one of the managing directors asked if he could join us. He said it was great to see me but treated me like he always had. That was pretty much the norm, and life at work began again.

Don't get me wrong. I didn't snap back into it instantly. My energy was still terrible. I had little to no confidence and felt completely overwhelmed. The combination of depression, lack of energy, no confidence and more medication made it tough for me to get out of bed. Many days I'd get up at 7 a.m. to let the dog out only to crawl back onto the couch until 10 or 11.

My boss at the time could not have been any better to me. He basically told me to do what I had to do and let him know if he could help. I remember one particular Friday afternoon I didn't go in the office until after 1 p.m. I stopped in his office and he just said, "Hey, you doing OK?" I said, "Yes," and that was it. Meanwhile my friends who also happen to report to me were as supportive as ever. They knew I'd be late but usually worked late to try and do as much as I thought I could. I couldn't have asked for better people to help me through this time. I will be grateful for them for the rest of my life.

27

"Balance"

That last slow recovery from depression hung on through October but, by the holidays, I was feeling as close to my version of normal as I had in a long time. I remember working the week between Christmas and New Year's as I didn't feel right taking "vacation." I officially had the days since the disability time didn't count against them, but I just couldn't do it. That was one sign that I was returning to my old self, considering I had spent a number of months dreading going to work.

During that week I could feel myself getting fully back into the groove of work. I started generating my own projects to work on and not just doing what I had to do to get by. More importantly, I started laughing and having fun again at work.

December (2010) became January and then February, and I was back to me again. That's when probably the best thing that could have happened to me happened. My psychiatrist quit. Don't get me wrong, he was a great guy, and he didn't quit because of me. At least I hope not! But I did get referred to his counterpart down the hall, who actually specializes in bipolar disorder.

In my first meeting with him, the new doctor looked at the medication I was on and said, "None of this will actually stop you from continuing to struggle with bipolar." All I did was stare at him like he had just read my death sentence. He continued by saying that I currently only had antidepressants to try and stop the depression or basement of the illness. I needed a "ceiling" to go with it. I knew what that ceiling would be: lithium. And I was right.

So I had come full circle. When I first had my battles with bipolar, I finally got the upper hand when I started taking lithium. Fourteen years later, it's back. My doctor said he has been doing this for a lot of years now and, if you can tolerate the drug, it's the best thing for bipolar. The old me wanted to resist as I've always had some stigma in my head regarding lithium. But I got over that quickly and took the prescription. That was about a year ago now, and the waves have smoothed out.

I don't have any exciting stories to tell you from the last year outside of being happy with my wife, enjoying my life and trying to appreciate every day. I take lithium and two other drugs every day. The competitive side of me would like to think I'm strong enough to handle this without medication, but the sensible side of me will win this argument from here on.

So that's my story, at least how I remember it. If you are struggling with bipolar or know someone who is, things can get better if you get help. You can't do it yourself. It has taken me a long time to accept what I have, and even longer to understand that it doesn't define who I am. It's like dealing with anything else in life. You just need to find balance.